The Phoenix Living Poets

POEMS

The Phoenix Living Poets

A COMMON GRACE
Norman MacCaig

THE WORLD I SEE
Patric Dickinson

SOME MEN ARE BROTHERS
D. J. Enright

WHEN THAT APRIL
Gillian Stoneham

POEMS
Lotte Zurndorfer

TIME FOR SALE
Edward Lowbury

SELECTED POEMS
James Merrill

THE SUN MY MONUMENT
Laurie Lee

FAIRGROUND MUSIC
John Fuller

THE RE-ORDERING OF THE STONES
Jon Silkin

CONTROL TOWER
Richard Kell

THE SWANS OF BERWICK
Sydney Tremayne

WORDS FOR BLODWEN
Gloria Evans Davies

ADDICTIONS
D. J. Enright

A ROUND OF APPLAUSE
Norman MacCaig

POEMS

by

ALEXANDER BAIRD

CHATTO AND WINDUS

THE HOGARTH PRESS

1963

Published by
Chatto and Windus Ltd
with The Hogarth Press Ltd
42 William IV Street
London WC2

Clarke, Irwin and Co. Ltd
Toronto

Acknowledgements

Acknowledgements are due to the following publications:

'The Texas Quarterly' for *Dry Summer*
'The London Magazine' for *Moon-viewing and Professor Kou, To My Wife, Mark Six or Seven Thoughts, That Lonely Heath, Year's End*
New Poems – 1960 (Hutchinson) for *Seat by an Open Window*
New Poems – 1962 (Hutchinson) for *Fire in November*

Contents

Dry Summer	9
Dark Background	10
Moon-Viewing and Professor Kou	11
Hiroshima Sunset	12
A Concern with Place	14
Myth–Making	16
Seat by an Open Window	17
Fire in November	19
To My Wife	20
May Evening	21
Flux	22
Mark Six or Seven Thoughts	23
That Lonely Heath	24
The Sleeper	25
The Secret Lover	26
Earth Tremor at Night	27
Love to the Japanese	28
In a Corner	30
Figures on a Ricefield	31
The Reverend Mr. Jones	32
Inmates out for an Airing	33
A Historian Eating Dates	34
The Foreigner and the Frog	35
Basket-worm	36
The Rain is Falling	38
Fall of Nature	40
Terrapin in a Hibachi	41
Shinto Shrine in Snow	42
Encounter with the Unconscious	44
Out of Sight of Land	45
Pastorale	47
Year's End	48

Dry Summer

God knows, there is no way to sit this out
Until the clownish cuckoo's exit line.
Like a brown trout's leap on slow waters
Was Spring's coming, but Summer –
Summer is a silence of all birds,
Summer is serious, all smeared with lime
To trap the fluttering boy, all birds with beaks full,
With only a second for the eye to aim
And line up love in the nick of time.

Through moths' wings of dusty curtains
My window from the Library looks
At sunlight stripping the azaleas
And girl students talking by
Walls of the new premises that sweat.
My chair squeals and the blind-cord twists itself –
Bookworms in love, I think – and break a fingernail
Desperate to open my window on the world,
In hope one more attempt will match
Beast with brain, one more dry summer
Send that flame searching through my thatch.

Dark Background

In Japan so many butterflies are black,
The largest crescent-winged like swallows, so
That when one settles on me I draw back
Repressing a tremor and expecting a blow.

I recognize here each familiar season
And yet I would not earth my face
Here as in my native place.
God keeps some instincts out of reach of reason.

When I was young my country was the park
With high prison walls enclosing hot
Seats where lovers writhed between
Shrubbery of laughing Indians unseen
And dry beds of dog-watered roses.

The kestrel-haunted cemetery towers
And blackbirds triumphing where the dead lie
Under jamjar vases of dead flowers,
Night of the clothes moth, day of the cabbage butterfly,
Were once my nature. There I found,
Orphaned perhaps from cage and packet seed,
A goldfinch mad with thistle-greed
Scattering tufted heads on sooty ground.

I have traversed the earth halfway across and down
And found no brightness that could skin the eye
Like the surprise of that child-tempting town.

Moon-Viewing and Professor Kou

      Yellow old
Oriental moon on your couch of needles,
You are not beautiful without help of pine
And tall grasses; and that you cannot be mine,
Wrinkled moon no longer intact and never unsung,
But that you seem his coeval makes him bold.

      Festival moon, do you
Illuminate Professor Kou in the garden where
He muses upon Wordsworth in his own tongue,
And are you always his inexpressible, true
And native moon? Then does he share
With you the deeper truths he keeps from me?

Grey moon, discover what I may not see.
For either he is wise enough, as I am not,
To read the brush-strokes on your Japanese face,
Or simply he is still unsure of what
I know, and seeks to keep me in my place.

In Japanese egotism there is a cult
Of the moon, which differs from any moon elsewhere,
And their humility, as easy to insult
As arrogance, is never slow to give a name
To native virtues for the stranger's sake . . .

      But there
Lies the Japan I cannot bring myself to blame.

Hiroshima Sunset

Abroad again among new sights, I find
This newness strange, where few old things remain,
Green rice fresh grown, the mountain slopes behind
New wooded since the day of deadly rain;
So now it is like any other city
That has identity outside the brain.

The city mantles. Twilight neon signs
Illuminate us and we smile at the winged thoughts
Trapped in the clinging webs of our designs.
Already I can see a sharp moon raking
Blue pine tops on the mountains, and a range
Of cloud summits topped with the
    daylight's last green flare.
Only the dead are earth whose colour does not change.
Buildings grow as we watch them; while we weigh
Our words, in earthquakes they may fall on us,
In quiet streets overpower us,
All our dooms are of their making.

It seems, when the sun sets, that orange glaciers run
Down to this street where broken hours are met;
They say the labouring women,
    skin charred by the sun,
Were many of them victims, and are yet.
Their red light glows. The city with a past
Blushes for us. Black-waggoned night
Will pick up all of us at last,
The dust we stir up sink into the ground
With tears and flesh and all that has become
Of past times, and the future will confound
Hiroshima with Herculaneum.

Living, I want to halt the sunset with a fan
Like Taira, and find some spot where
    Plato would have stood
To judge the whole dispassionately, yet without
Neglect of parts, since souls are fragments of the Good.

A Concern with Place

When I think of the years' wasting I think of being
Involved with war before I knew and
Nineteen or twenty when I first saw Babylon,
A spot where Euphrates, river of life,
    took an unpredicted
Turn, the start of my occupation with places.
I make that my Carthage, ashes and
    bloody clay transmuted,
Of the third book of my confessions:
Bitter ashes becoming paste for the ceramist,
The Author of indestructible impressions,
Clay being baked brick on the processional avenue
Not unlike the alleys where echoes of childhood feet
Still shudder from wall to wall, but this was full
Of lion, improbable sirrush,* and bull.

A baked tablet riddled over with cuneiform
Fixed me running up the ziggurat† where once
The god priest sat tumescent in the upper coolness
And felt his vigour returning after the sacred act.
I did not stoop to take the tablet but ran on
Boyishly up that portentous scree of shards.
And since till then I had not known knowledge denied,
I asked for a key to those symbols on the ground.
'Such as you have no concern with what they say.'
Dismissed by the education officer on my station –
And yet today I am not so easily turned away –
But quite consoled when I took the
    Plutarch from my kitbag,

sirrush the commonly supposed name of a mythical monster
    depicted on the bas-reliefs of Babylon.
†*ziggurat* an ancient Babylonian temple-mound.

Seat by an Open Window

It was in the March month and all appeared
Uneasy as water and distrustful of the sun.
I had demolished what in winter had passed for
Cloud-cuckoo-land to find myself still hedged
In by imposing tables and straddling chairs,
Among which the voices of women in the street
Intruded uninvited; voices complaining
Made the tour of my furniture. But I
Can close no window on any tones that promise
Revelations, nor ever could. I tell you again,
There was no place for me to be but where you stood.

Phrases wandered round my walls, to drown
In cushions, echo from plaster. They underlined
The irony of the inanimate, that quality
That forbids us to unmake it, and we obey
Since we dare not interfere with Things.
So then I let myself be tied by ropes of thought,
Of thinking instead of seeing – but to think of you
Was all that I wanted then – wishing instead of being.

I waited in my chair and, as the day
Swelled, other sounds fell in upon me: steps
And cries and wheels. I did not look to see
If those had gone (I think they had) but still
The voices were around me, settled in
Against my will and part of my possessions.
It is like this always in March when we open windows
On days that are falsely fine. And yet I tell you,
I wished to hear no voice but yours. No fault but mine

If I waited – I will not say for what – only trusting
In the promise of revelations. Then I looked around
My room and from the window; mistaken if I expected
Your shadow on that daylight's apse of dazzling tinsel.
The place and time were wrong, those voices marred
My mood. Restless I opened and closed my books;
The sounds flew out of them like moths and dust
Leaving a desolation, an afternoon passed unobserved,
Long hours let go in the waste of an anticipation.

Fire in November

This is your ground and mine. Tread soft, replace the lock.

Within a few hours the heat has risen twenty degrees
After numb night, and now we know that we exist.
The shrike signals from telephone wire to the gaudy
Incontinent redstart, who is never at ease,
That we walk in this garden which is ticking like a clock
As small seeds burst out of a dried up cyst
And two grass stems, crippled by frost, relax.

This is late autumn in Japan, with most trees
Leafless and only the evergreens bright by carp ponds
And the maples like red weals on the mountains' backs.

This is the warning of cold, an autumn of the flesh
Daunts us, but that is far away. Who knows
What will have replaced it before that time?
Of course we cannot imagine alternatives, of course
Summer is everlasting; Eros eludes the lime.

Blue smoke. Somewhere our neighbour is burning leaves.
Ours still lie, dappled like antique earthenware,
Unharvested fall. The trip from you to me
Is short, but they hide our pathway through this garden
To which the irreverent sun has a master key
And amiable sundials count only the hours we choose.

Here we stroll secure from little dragons' barking
And the wonders beyond the Wall. For once I do not care
If now our neighbour is walking barefoot on his embers.

This is your ground and mine,
        the minute that one remembers.

To My Wife

What new day has blown in now
Gusty with dust and doubt?
         He looks the same
As any other. Close the door.
Time-trailed like you and me,
     he knows there's no way out.

But what if he were what we both
Suspect, what if now
         while the last
Owl's shriek still shivers twigs, a white
Inhuman hand should pass us
     both that golden bough

Which lets us in on the secret? Our
May mornings still bring visions
         and the turf
Still dances to our heels. Before the blood
Grows yellow as a leaf,
     we've small time for decisions.

'Time and to spare,' the ghosts intone,
But we are not deceived.
         (They'd make us theirs.)
Our heads are not our own, if this
Is not our day, and hearts
     are not to be believed.

May Evening

On May Day when I opened the white front door
And the fly screen cluttered with the dead
At ten fifteen at night, a sound of cicadas
Jarred me like love. A whiteness on the trunk
Of the dying cherry tree was a powder
To discourage termites, but the illusion of snow
Lying was too luxurious to forgo.
Not even termite powder shall escape me in May.

Flux

Not love, simplicity might have
    escaped us though,
Had any goatish stroller come
On you and me an hour ago.
Were we not married there'd be some
Excuse for us. No medievalist,
Mind full of young man and maid,
Gold May morning and green glade,
But would forgive us, were we not
Married. But so we are and what
We celebrate in this half-furtive style
Is that your eyelids and your smile
Still allow this green world to exist.

With beaks for lips and scaly feet we might
Feel less stranger-like. What flux can I use
To fix this moment in this place, to fuse
With the world our host love this parasite?
Don't swear, you say, and make no
    compact with what's past
For one May, one yellow morning's sake,
Since what will fuse you with the world will take
One away from two, and must at last.

Mark Six or Seven Thoughts

Mark six or seven thoughts at dusk and let them loose
Before the tentacled sun dying stains earth black,
Thoughts bright as fish and one perhaps will find me out
In labyrinths of dimly-lit aquaria
Where fantasies glide open-mouthed behind the glass.

Mark six or seven thoughts at midnight, when both sound
And silence startle, set them free at what cold time
You take your white face in the mirror for a ghost's.
While yet I am most near no thought can reach me, though
Mine is the ghost reflection hints at in your glass.

Mark six or seven thoughts at dawn and set them free
Over the burnished lakes and landmarks of the sky
Soft-winged as owls, and I shall listen for their cries
Borne on the wind that is your breath, out of the mist
Of incommunicable words breathed on to glass.

Loose six or seven thoughts at noon, and, if one reach
Me, mirrors have no need of light, nor love of speech.

That Lonely Heath

On this heath for you and me no meeting place,
No fire-fed hut, no hands warmed
    where the beak of frost
Teased the flames like cockerels' tails,
    and grey wool rolled
Adrift as light as blue down lost
In mist, where ash like lace,
Discoloured, crumbled old.

The fire is out, where once a mask of heat
Rippled without the wind,
Shadows ambitiously grew tall,
Broad, bold enough to disappear.
A log coughed and collapsed;
    the new moon grinned
Through glass; fire died with
    neither of us here.

But sometimes I – and you, I think – arrange
Small journeys to this well-forgotten place
To see this heath, the hut that stood alone
But flame-bright with another's face –
And how that looked when it was strange
And less well known.

The Sleeper

Nimble tomorrow has found the crack in the door;
Inquisitive tomorrow looks on her asleep,
On her closed eyes as sweet as
    honey-jars and deep,
And his lost innocence too soon aware of sin
Knows that if he breaks the lock she is no more.

Watchful tomorrow is looking for a way in.

When I awake she will not be like this:
The skin changed, constant substitution of the flesh.
Some small thing will have changed in her
    and winds blow fresh
Through a blind night of searching
    for the thing I miss.

It touches *me*, that precious part of everyone
Sleep loses, like some wisdom none
    but she can find –
Lost, the irrecoverable rhythm gone
Where we repay earth's hospitality in kind.

The Secret Lover

You and I practise secret love. I kiss your face
In a small room, for public love is a disgrace.

There is peace only when we two are alone.
Our age of gold, where you and I are
    knocked down and sold,
Our middle age, for past and future are out of reach,
May prove as dark as the last, until our native speech
Lies back content with yielding no Rosetta Stone.

With it will die the strangeness
    of our thought, that free
And captive worlds exist only in you and me.

Yesterday the beloved king, this morning a still thing,
Last week the elected head of government, today dead.
The great go every day, quiet or drugged stupid,
From blind shots at chipped brick walls,
From rope and the cheap chair kicked aside.

And the lord of life became a chubby cupid
About the time that the last civilization died.

Earth Tremor at Night

So you expect me to know the answer to all questions
Merely because I answer something in you. No
Wise man reveals all his knowledge. Be resigned
To having an inkling only of where love is inclined
And let this soft white ocean remain uncharted.

Tonight there were stars; how many neither of us knows.
One does not count them like stars painted on a screen;
Like sudden glimpses of the empyrean they
Lick hot through heaven's holes and it can be seen
How one may hide from the moon but not from those.

So the fire of stars can reach us on earth here,
Whether we reach for them or not; but I
Dissociate myself from all such strivings.
Come, you and I together make up a perfect sphere.
Our crystal globe enfolds more globes like a Chinese box,
And why should we wish to hide? There's none to say
You and I must not make this oldest kind
Of heavenly music for each other's sake.

But what is this thunder and why does the earth shake?
Now do you feel a want of sympathy for the wise?
Since you are my earth-shaker, you will find
That sometimes I see things with a child's eyes
And there is much you may have to explain.
Be patient at that time; I have no plan
For dodging truth or acting as the simple man.

Love to the Japanese

Before I came I had not guessed they were Romantics;
But on the hill up to the rustic shrine
Above the sacred sakaki branches two canes stand.
When the wind hums they sway mysteriously in concert.
Eyes of small children watch me from behind a bush.

On my return I see them again and from a bough
A wooden cage small enough for a pet cicada
And in it a green bird hopping, hopping.
    I guess the secret:
There is a fine black net between the bamboo canes,
And the incident reminds me of Theocritus.

A bird-catcher, still but a boy,
    while hunting in a patch
Of wood, caught sight of Eros
    the elusive sitting there
Upon a box-tree bough and, welcoming the
    chance to catch
So fine a bird, he fixed his canes at once
    and tried to snare
Love, who lightly dodged him here
    and there till, sick at heart
Because his tackle failed, the poor boy
    threw his canes aside.

He sought the ancient ploughman
    who had first taught him his art,
Told him his tale and showed him where
    Love sat. The sage replied,
Shaking his head and smiling,
    'Spare the creature. Run away
And leave this bird alone – it does no good.
    So long as you
Don't catch him you'll be perfectly content,
    but on the day
When you are come to man's estate
    this very creature who
Eludes you now, while your attempts to
    capture him are vain,
Will come and perch inside your head.
    You'll have him on the brain!'

The green, hopping trophy in the cage
    has a white eye-ring.
The children think it is a bush-warbler they have netted,
The Japanese nightingale, the spring's sweet singer.
I shall not tell them it is only a white-eye,
For in any case they will not let him go
And with this belief they will admire
    his poor song more.

In a Corner

In Tokyo strip shows, strip lighting, strip cartoons
Are as elsewhere, such restaurants as this in which
The world and his (adopted) daughter come my way;
He is in business, they are both in business.
Do not mind me sitting here. Tonight I am content to be
The looker-on, a spider at my table by the door.

That bright girl with the fingernails, what is she waiting for?
I met her eye a while since and it seemed an answer
Dropped with the soft down moulting from her cigarette.

He comes, snow-blinded by the knives and tablecloths,
Good-looking, Japanese, grey hairs undyed as with good taste,
To shipwreck on coral smiles – those lips away –
A well-dressed ghost, forgive him if . . . a shade too fond
For good; but if she were the devil she is blonde.

Sparked from blue eyes, steel-lidded, like a basinet
Her bright talk screens her mind. So cultured mosses mask
The bound feet of this potted palm. I meet her eye
Again, but the engaged tone tells me no reply.

He is a little older than I and certainly richer.
I am not apt to despise the real values. No,
But had I a madman's leisure I might trace his life
Growing bolder and balder with each stroke of the comb
Till some humiliation sends him to his wife.

If I had a madman's wit – those eyes away –
I could twist my anguished fingers in my hair,
But I must wait till I am old and dare.

Figures on a Ricefield

An old man wades with a girl carrying chrysanthemums,
Stooped, so old that all his will has turned to wish,
An old man walking heron-like in shallow water,
For like the young rice piercing the surface of the mirror
The legs of both are lengthened by a trick of light.

Behind his eyes he knots a net to catch bright fish,
Speculation, the mind's fine mesh without a rift;
The catch he offers to no one but his grand-daughter,
Thoughts worthy of no ear that is not dutiful.

So age is a boat in which old men are cut adrift,
For the girl looks at her flowers' reflections, and her eyes
Are tangled in one concept of the beautiful,
Nose, mouth, the singular conjunction of her face.

She recognizes how her own dark lashes curl;
She is a moon princess and moves in another place
Where no old man wastes wisdom on a little girl.

The Reverend Mr. Jones

'Ninety next month.' He smiles
　　with eyes that do not see
As he quotes Homer on our
　　hostess pouring tea;
Most of his talk of masters,
　　senior fellows, least
Of bishops and the Church,
　　though he has been a priest.

Departing, he is lifted heavy
　　from his chair;
Nice reference to Horace and
　　'I must go now
Back to the Home and my
　　poached egg.' Stick gropes for stair.

Oh bright head, age-browned skin,
　　opaque eyes, how
Long before the baser setting
　　rots around
The gem and intellect falls
　　naked to the ground?

Pinned on his finer points of
　　scholarship, I writhe
Still fumbling for my Greek.
　　Death, savour your fat fill
Of earthly frame and fame.
　　I think that minds as lithe
As whips, like lizards' tails
　　lash after flesh is still.

Inmates out for an Airing

We walk together,
    but each in his own
Crystal compartment of small
    thoughts mutters and is alone.

This shadow on my left hand is
    my friend who died one day
A year ago. You see his
    hair is grey.
His lizard shadow slithers over
    sandstone walls.
Sometimes I stop, but never hear
    where his foot falls.
He walks always behind my head,
    one year away.

Do not be afraid to meet my eye;
    I am not proud.
We are out for a walk in the sun,
    each by himself in a crowd.
Each is real among the shadows,
    plump among the wizened, new
Among the old. Look.
    Teach me to believe in you.
Tell me you are not a shadow.
    Take my hand; pretend
To be my equal.
    All my wisdom is aware
Of your forgetting, and my head's
    no place to spend
A life in; but it's you who find
    this hard to bear.

(Lancaster Moor Hospital)

A Historian Eating Dates

He has a taste for counting time
In reverse and chasing up
Back numbers of the centuries
In mouldering calendars. He finds
His dates come mixed with circumstance
And dead men's judgments. Clarified,
These yield up facts, and so he takes
Some pleasure in the heavy work –
Unnatural selection. I,
For one, prefer the sweet and soiled
Flesh of the fruit; he saves the stone.

He sees in this a potency
Which excites him. And I too
Can guess at the analogy:
Out of the stone a palm can grow,
The sacred precinct where each kills
The priest before him and then reigns
Secure, so long as theories live.

Flesh of the fruit. Not that I ask
For all, but part of it, a taste,
A little something to remind
Me of myself, the element
Of human will for good or ill,
The common theme that tongues wear out.

The Foreigner and the Frog

After rice-planting, when the girls were singing,
I saw a frog in the paddy field, dying and dumb,
As if a child were afloat on a lava lake –
Such a child as I had seen dancing solemn with delight
Within a circle of red cheeks, each burning bright
As the summer lanterns, with small handclasps ringing
An old man with a drum.

Mud still astir from the planting ceremony
Bore the frog helpless to where I stood.
He struggled in mud like a sleeper who could not shake
The dream off. Then he was safe beside me. I don't know
How he'd escaped the mud-harrow's teeth, the slow
Plodding of bullocks' twisted hoofs. But seeing through
Long grass my stranger's face, he turned and fell
Back into the doom he knew, the familiar hell.
For we are not all brothers in this land where race
Has meaning and the devil wears a foreign face.

In the land of cherries Issa made a poem about a frog,
Seeing a beauty under clammy skin and when
He looked at popped eyes guessing a truth behind.
The cherry petals fall down gently on drunken men
But this I cannot understand, having an alien mind.
For we are not all brothers – though God knows we try –
With those faces under the cherries, the frog, Issa and I.

Basket-worm

The piece-of-eight moon that rolls across
A plum-red, ripening sky observes
Your dereliction swinging from a twig,
A rag-bag dangling from a bare cherry tree,
Worn leaves sutured to the obscure purpose
Of a dreaming grub. Tomorrow is
The first day of the year of the patient Ox.

I congratulate you on your adherence.
This morning a little snow still clung to you
As you swung round and round loosely
Like an old witch on a gallows-tree.
Who shall see the moment of your awakening?

Probably I shall not. It seems that I
Have no use for symbols at this age.
Still for me you are taut with pain not passion,
For I have identified you and your silence.
The mummy might have spoken once from sand,
That in the labelled case is for ever dumb.

The thing about Chinese characters is that once
Learnt they are seen everywhere. Not merely
In neon signs for *sake* and bicycles,
But in the incongruous association
Of twisted trees and telegraph poles,
Of scaffolding sprawled bone-idle on half-built walls.

And clouds. Clouds are the best of all, they bear
The bold, authentic brush-marks of the wind.
But in you I see the potency of the germ:
No word, but a conspiracy among twigs.
Later all may be legible; now is too soon.

The young are force-fed on symbols. I know I ought
To take a stick and knock you down, but I
Lack the courage to kill. Oh, you look dead
Now – but when the rag-bag is broken,
What pale thing will be seen to squirm inside
Like a bird's embryo in a fallen egg?

By old custom we are all a year older
Tomorrow under heaven. Tonight the moon
Glares like a falcon's yellow eye.
Caught on my gauntlet time begins to bate . . .
And the wind rocks you kindly. You are thoughts
Unread; I must not touch you now. Too late.

The Rain is Falling

The rain is falling in this poem.
Seven days' wind blew from the east
    in parched cold;
Now rain comes, shrunken fingers
    of ghosts at the window.
The pallid soil which was frozen
    this afternoon
Is now sodden. Rain is falling
    as cars go past
Hissing like snakes, or insects
    trapped by a sun shower
Who, doomed to fly on,
    their buzzing slightly damped,
Will not settle for fear
    wet wings will stick
To glass or stone and the hot,
    treacherous sun
Return to roast them chained there.
    Cars are passing.

Rain is falling in their
    drivers' bad dreams,
In at their off-side windows,
    on to windscreens.
Slate roofs are become
    sleek and black again
And the dry crusts in the yard
    will swell,
And pigeons will go clapping
    up from them
As the knob of the yellow
    back-door turns.

Somewhere the rain is dripping
    like a footstep.
Now wooden huts are streaked
    like sparrows' backs.
Wires have begun to rust
    and wood to rot
Imperceptibly. Since the dry
    curtains start to fall,
Tomorrow the unexplained patch
    will be on the wall.

Rain will be falling in our
    sleep (though we
Shall lie, arms over each other,
    forgetting it.)
Rain falling with improbable rhythms
On to window-sills, like the
    hard thought
With a sharp cutting edge that
    divides men,
Like the adamant of the soul
    that passes through
Our flimsier existence.
    Upon such nights
In darkness we are convinced
    we heard a Voice
And as easily persuaded that
    there was none,
Only the easy inexplicable rain.

Fall of Nature

As we climb to where the mountain priests found
The truth once, and no longer need to look around,
In an oak leaf's centre a small, green frog
Swells like a goblin, seeming about to float away
Blown up with wisdom.

        Now we hear
From the mountainside sweating with morning fog
Machine-gun chatter, as a falcon stoops
To the airy conquest of a stray kite,
And voices that philosophy cannot come near
Of country-women arguing in knee-deep groups
Planting rice in terraced paddies.

        Lonely,
Hurrying, armoured in emerald and grey,
A tiger beetle runs before us to excite
A dollar-green snake, whose eyes must
    behold the light.

Two metres long, four fingers thick, it leaves no trail
But crosses the hard path in a panic only
One shudder ahead of us. The serpent-tail
Runners of the dwarf bamboo alarm us now,

Till we come to where a boulder leans, below
Which some saint sat for too long, for that is how
This search began, this discontent with what we know.

Terrapin in a Hibachi

Terrapin in a fire-bowl, floating like a magic island,
You turn your ancient bird-head up to me
As if you sought the answer to the phoenix riddle.
In nature there are not so many curious things,
If we think rightly. Only a narrow sophistication
Lets us suppose a praying mantis is surprising.
The real oddities are these things that have no name;
For we seize our chance when nature seems to allow
A liberty – with hybrids of such quaint devising.
This terrapin, water and fire-bowl show that we,
Like earthenware, can have no part in nature now.

Let you and I, shopkeeper, look at nature frankly –
I take it that you own both bowl and terrapin.
We thought we tamed her long ago, and this is especially
True in Japan. And yet she roars more loudly here
Where *waka* and *haiku* bottle her like a djinn.
Have you considered the explosive quality
Of this compound, would you have us all rethink?
Wise men like you and me are old before their time
And have things too soon pat. I write in praise
Of folly, you invoke the fiery terrapin,
Both confident that we cannot be touched by them.

Terrapin floating in the fire-bowl like an island,
You turn your ancient bird-head up to me
As if that secret still eluded you,
Knowing only the bounds of your cold bowl of oceans
And an old brick that is your continental shelf.
There is no secret, I at least keep nothing from you.
I know this is your trick to have me see myself
Some decades from now remembering the entire
Picture, you and a bowl that ought to be filled with fire.

Shinto Shrine in Snow

Nuthatch and titmouse flicker among cedars and fly
From ice-knives dropping as a fresh branch cracks.
We trace the beaten snow path; someone strays
And a soft whiteness clasps him to the thigh.
Such pitfalls warn us not to follow the rabbits' tracks.

We climb the squeaking slope,
    black-booted as mountaineers,
And near the summit snow flares with the orange rays
Shed by painted pillars under an olive-green
Roof of cypress bark. We walked too long, we said,
By grey cliffs, twisted pines, and frozen waterfalls,
A series of flat pictures in the snow convention.
Now this: the warm shock of the unexpected sight
More typical of this land,
    the burning third dimension
Leads us to reinterpret sober and well bred
Taste which admits a double meaning of the Mean
Against the spectrum, crude complexion of pure light.

Because we dupe ourselves with breadth of mind,
I can understand, one says and dares the others
To a denial, holding out as at arm's length
For admiration the thought that all
    beliefs are brothers.
Let us admit it, seeing more than we wish to see;
All this vermilion is beyond our comprehension.
We cannot guess what this spot means to the straw-shod,
Straw-shouldered mountain people, what old faith
Is drawn to this old cedar forest by some half god
Wolf-eyed in betrayed woman's or fox's guise.

42

Shall we look for a priest inside? and, Which was here
First, the shrine or the god of the grove? and,
　　Imagination –
Pace the artist – needs to be met more than halfway!
We say, as if to sell our souls for the broader view.

At any moment some shorn ghost may ring that bell
Which hangs silent and green above blue-drifted ground.
A timber slung horizontally almost touches it,
So that a child's hand could swing it into urgent sound.
But with the clamour who may appear? No, come away.
Silence shall break into voices, but this is not the day.
The fearless rabbits race on these white slopes at night
And we plod here in terror at the noon's height.

Encounter with the Unconscious

A dark pool among giant bamboos and
    ousels' cries,
Azure demoiselles, yellow and brown dragonflies,
And a sudden frightening splash –
Of fish? I seemed to see a drowned face in the water.
Black and blue butterflies battered
    the air at its magic edge.

Cobwebs appearing with a slender flash
Of silver, like apparitions creeping thin between
Wooden, unpainted wall and paper screen
To swell into a third dimension
Of horror, stickily stroked my cheek.

But when I came back by the same path
A new quiet had replaced that first alarm
And while I searched the haunted ground
For an explanation, far out
On a tree submerged in that devils' bath
But poking up one shrivelled, bare-bone arm
A terrapin comically clung. Peering about,
He saw me like a spirit coming after
Him, and shyly plopped into familiar water.

The only way to treat ghosts is with laughter.

Out of Sight of Land

Swimming in crimson light
  the forecastle throws blue shadows.
In and out of ropes and wires
  the sea breeze sings.
But none of these is life,
  only the phosphorescent
Green disks spinning under the bow
  are living things.

Here outlines blur; what shadows
  just now in the stern
Were men, perhaps that brown-finned
  shark-god could have said,
Captured just off Sumatra,
  brave but how soon dead!

Somewhere in sleep the small birds
  stir which came aboard
At the last port. In darkness
  someone speaks, yet these
Are not life, but the momentary
  shapes of thought.

I find night's constellations changed;
  familiar forms
Are fallen out of sight.
  The moon is not the same –
Pallid, a friend with eyes
  unnaturally bright.

Sun, you are no one. Shall I too
    fall in that snare?
Sun, did I bring you from an
    English sky with me
Out of the chastening and
    decent veil of fogs
To watch you like a lover
    letting your red hair
Down on a flying-fish and
    seabird dimpled sea?

On such evenings respectable
    women are for flinging
Discretion over the side
    and grey priests
Dream of the next port
    and honey-skinned Eurasians;

Because this floating island
    is not of today or tomorrow,
But out of yesterday it came bringing
Forgotten and unregretted-till-now occasions
Let slip. Time is progress overland,
But the ocean dissolves such preconceptions
And which of time's monuments
    can we understand
Except by this landmark and that?
    Here are no landmarks.

Year's End

The nibbling year of the Rat has almost won
Its caucus race from oysters to persimmons
In this region famed for both.
    The first month's clawprints,
Stars pressed in the snow,
    with a comet's streak between,
Will soon appear again as the Rat year passes.

Now the catcalls of kites
    idling black against blue,
With, from the pines,
    the high hag-cackle of the shrike,
Speed him, and the panicky roar of the Ox
Kneedeep in mud, who will inherit the new year
But sees the Tiger not fourteen months away.

Though we infest time with our images, hanging
A paper mask on the death's head, bone must last
Like the Ox and Rat beyond the new year's cards
And the Tiger is always a tiger even on paper.

Pastorale

A hecatomb to some forgotten god
Muddies my lane; oxen of shambling gait
For queenly Juno. Loudvoiced a labourer
Manhandles cattle past my lichened gate.

Shrill grasses windwhipped
    scar the stream with white
Clawing the surface pouting fishlips ring;
The dog nips heifers' heels by woodland where
The yaffles' peals of loony laughter ring.

A barnowl, nightwhite, shrieks an elfin spell
To freeze all mice; roostready rooks alight
Where elm twigs, crisscross kindling, rub the sun
And for a breath the clouds are set alight.

The long grass prickles
    with shrews' pineneedling voices
And small birds mutter watching daylight die.
So aging poets are moved again to try
Odes in old modes, a last cast of the die.